My King, My Lover, My Friend
（大王、爱人、朋友）

A Book of Poetry and
Autobiographical Commentary

**P. J. Guidera,
A Servant of the Most High God**

WESTBOW
P R E S S®
A DIVISION OF THOMAS NELSON
& ZONDERVAN

This book is a work of non-fiction. Unless otherwise noted, the author and the publisher make no explicit guarantees as to the accuracy of the information contained in this book and in some cases, names of people and places have been altered to protect their privacy.

Scripture quotations taken from the Holy Bible, New Living Translation, Copyright © 1996, 2004. Used by permission of Tyndale House Publishers, Inc., Wheaton, Illinois 60189. All rights reserved.

Scripture quotations are from The Holy Bible, English Standard Version® (ESV®), copyright © 2001 by Crossway, a publishing ministry of Good News Publishers. Used by permission. All rights reserved.

WestBow Press books may be ordered through booksellers or by contacting:

WestBow Press
A Division of Thomas Nelson & Zondervan
1663 Liberty Drive
Bloomington, IN 47403
www.westbowpress.com
1 (866) 928-1240

Because of the dynamic nature of the Internet, any web addresses or links contained in this book may have changed since publication and may no longer be valid. The views expressed in this work are solely those of the author and do not necessarily reflect the views of the publisher, and the publisher hereby disclaims any responsibility for them.

Any people depicted in stock imagery provided by Thinkstock are models, and such images are being used for illustrative purposes only. Certain stock imagery © Thinkstock.

ISBN: 978-1-5127-0595-9 (sc)
ISBN: 978-1-5127-0596-6 (hc)
ISBN: 978-1-5127-0594-2 (e)

Library of Congress Control Number: 2015912252

Print information available on the last page.

WestBow Press rev. date: 08/13/2015

For the One Who sacrificed His Life on my behalf.
You are My Greatest Pursuit and My Truest Love.

For Deidre Terry.
A faithful wife, a loving mother, and a
most excellent woman of God.

And for my wife, who, as of yet, is still unknown to me.
You are constantly in my prayers,
and I wait patiently and longingly for
the LORD to make us one.

Contents

Introduction

There is tremendous power in words. They can either build or destroy, either give life or take it away. Jesus said, "The words that I have spoken to you are spirit and life."[1] And James tells us in chapter 3, verses 1-12 of his epistle that we can control our whole body if we can control the words we speak. These, and many other examples throughout the Bible, display the power of words whether they come from the Mouth of God or from human mouths. And so, it is critical that we learn to use this power with discipline and self-control in a manner honoring to the One who created all things by His Word. In regards to this book specifically, it is my hope that the words I present will be powerful and will greatly impact your perspective on life and on the God we Christians claim to serve. I hope the words I have chosen will be bring clarity and understanding when God and His ways seem confusing and beyond comprehension. And I hope by reading these words your love and appreciation for Our Author are strengthened, but, more importantly,

---

[1] John 6:63b (ESV)

that your appreciation for how much He loves *you* is deepened.

I remember when the idea for this book came to me. It was about two and a half years ago, late summer/early fall of 2012, right around the same time I began doing one-on-one discipleship with a great man of The Faith, Brock Fallon. By that time, my journaling and my poetry writing had gotten pretty serious and had become a consistent part of my relationship with The King as I "work[ed] out [my] salvation in fear and trembling."[2] However, up to that point, I had never even considered actually sitting down, typing everything out, and seeking a publisher for my work. But when the LORD hits you with an idea, it's pretty unmistakable. The vision of what this book should be was so clear and so vivid in my mind even down to the style, the content, and the cover design, including the color scheme for the entirety of the book. To me, undeniable. "I must write this book," I thought to myself.

However, as I now sit down and actually begin to write this book, I can't help but be somewhat amused or even incredulous. I never thought of myself as someone capable of writing a book. I remember I always used to say, "I could never write a book. I simply do not have enough to say about any one subject to ever have the amount of material you would need to write one." Well,

---

[2] Philippians 2:12 (ESV)

surprise! I guess I do, in fact, have enough to say because here I am writing this. Or perhaps I should say the LORD has given me enough to say about Him, because I truly believe that this book is His idea, not mine.

It does seem rather fitting though. God enjoys using people in the exact ways they think they are most deficient. And those who know me well know that Jesus and the things of God are the only topics I ever really have much to say about. Thank you to all of my friends and family who confirmed this vision for me by encouraging me to continue writing and by asking me if I would ever try to publish anything. Your fellowship and godly examples are forever impressed onto my heart, mind, and soul. And a special thank you to all the members of the Body of Christ in Okinawa, Japan, with whom I had the honor and privilege of fellowshipping. A significant portion of the content of this book was inspired by or written during my two years of service there.

On the topic of content, before you, the reader, dive into the real meat and potatoes of this book, I would like to explain from where all these writings came. Every bit of this book can be found somewhere in my journals.[3] What you are about to read is my heart, mind, and soul poured out onto paper, with nothing less than glorifying and loving My Savior as the aim. The various pieces contained herein are a mixture of poems, commentaries,

---

[3] Or on my Facebook page. Haha.

essays, and prayers, with poems and their associated background commentaries making up the majority.

I started journaling while attending the Naval Academy. And the only reason why I started writing poetry was because I felt inspired by a young Chinese woman I had met during one of my summers abroad in Tianjin, China. (万一你看这本书，你就知道你是谁。我希望你将来懂得上帝多么爱你。Translation: "If by chance you read this book, you know who you are. I hope someday you will understand how much the Most High God loves you.") In fact, I had written several poems in Mandarin on behalf of this young lady long before I ever started writing anything in English to honor The King. It is interesting how He cultivates the gifts He has given each of us and what he uses to draw our attention to them. In this case, He knew I would pay attention to this young woman, and He knew that the feelings I felt toward her would inspire me for the first time to write my thoughts down in the form of poetry. Excepting the many things I learned about God, myself, the Chinese culture, and relationships, nothing ever came of the intimate friendship this young lady and I shared. But I believe the LORD got everything that He desired for me out of this experience. For it was this relationship that began to engage the gift of words with which I believe He has blessed me.

A couple of the poems presented within are written in Mandarin Chinese. Why? Because quite frankly, I have a tremendous amount of love for China: its language, its people, its history, and its culture. I remember when I was a little kid in elementary school history class. Besides the obsession that all little boys have with ninjas and samurai warriors (which I understand are not Chinese), I paid extra close attention whenever Asia was brought up. Something about the character-based writing systems, scroll paintings, and traditional architecture—which now I know is mostly from Tang Dynasty China—fascinated me. Later on, I began studying Chinese at the Naval Academy, and my general fascination with Asia started to become more specific to China. Then when I finally traveled to the country for the first time, I knew it was on.[4] I believe the passion, desire, and excitement I feel toward China are directly from the LORD. It is part of who He has designed me to be. Hence, where I am able, I use my gift of words in this beautiful language as well. Where the original poem is in Chinese, I have also included the English translation. Although, I would encourage the reader to learn some Mandarin, as I feel the Chinese better expresses the meaning which I wanted to convey in the poem. And for those of you who may read this who are native speakers of the language, if

---

[4] As I am writing this, it has been almost four years since my last visit. Genuinely and sincerely, this fact is the cause of occasional disappointment for me.

I totally butcher the use of your language, please accept my sincerest apologies. Just know that it was done out of appreciation and respect for your culture, not disdain or contempt.

Lastly, earlier in the introduction, I mentioned that I believe this book to be God's idea, not mine. Should the reader take this to mean I believe this book is "divinely inspired?" Yes. Perhaps not in the same sense as the Prophets of the Old Testament or the Apostles of the New Testament, but at least in the sense that all who have received the Holy Spirit have direct access to the Mind and Heart of the Living God. As my good friend and mentor, Brock Fallon, would say: "I am neither a prophet nor the son of a prophet." However, once you have accepted The Blood as payment for your sins and received the Holy Spirit, you become one with your Father in Heaven. I believe everything that follows is consistent with Biblical principles and with what Jesus the Christ has taught me about Himself through the guidance of the Holy Spirit, or, at the very least, is edifying and uplifting to the Body of Christ in a manner which is pleasing to Him.

Now, find a comfy chair or go to your favorite reading spot, and join me as I attempt to take you "higher up and deeper in."[5]

---

[5] C.S. Lewis

I

(NECESSITIES)

The poem that follows, interestingly enough, was finalized the same day I began writing this book. I originally started this poem several months earlier when I was still in Okinawa. I remember sitting in the Starbucks in American Village off Highway 58 when I came up with the idea for the poem. My initial concept seemed satisfactory. However, as I began putting pen to paper, it quickly got too wordy. The idea of the poem was to express the bare essentials for living a good life: what do we really need? This was the unstated question that positioned itself squarely in my mind as I wrote the poem. So, in the spirit of bare essentials, I wanted the verbiage to be simple, straightforward, and without excess. I got through the first few lines and had to stop; I didn't really like what I had written. I decided maybe that day just wasn't the right day to finish the poem. So I put my pen down, picked up the book I had been reading before my inspirational interruption, and left the poem partially written to be finished another time.

Fast forward several months, I was now living in Victorville, CA, after having executed permanent change of station orders to Marine Corps Logistics Base Barstow. Faced with re-establishing myself in America after living overseas for two years and with the task of furnishing a two-bedroom apartment on my own, the question—what do we really need?—found its way back to the forefront of my mind. The reason for this was very simple: money.

While I was in Okinawa, I was fortunate enough—or perhaps I should say blessed—to save up a very significant amount of money. So significant, in fact, that when I hit American soil, I had enough money to pay off the remaining balance of a loan I had taken out while at the Naval Academy, to buy a brand new Toyota Tacoma and a used Suzuki GSX-R600, and to have a few thousand left over. Wow. Thank you, Lord.

But money and I have a weird relationship. For one, because I don't like money. It's hard to be friends with someone you don't like. I like what I can do with money. But I don't like money itself. Money, for me, is like one of those coworkers you really only talk to when you want something from them. And two, because I am always worrying about whether or not I am using the money the LORD provides for me in a wise and appropriate manner. Sometimes I catch myself wanting to spend more money than I feel I should. When this happens, I ask myself, "Do I *need* this?" And more often than not, the answer is, "No, I don't need this." I will not die if I do not buy it. My friends and family will still support me if I do not have it. And most importantly, Jesus will still love me if I decide my money is best used elsewhere.

The question of need does not always determine whether I follow through on the purchase or not. After all, if I bought or possessed only what I actually need, my apartment and my person would look rather more sparse than they do currently. However, I ask the question of myself regardless because I want to make sure that, at the very least, I am consciously acknowledging my ability to get along just fine without making the forthcoming purchase. I want to keep all things in their proper perspective, and I want to keep my priorities in line with what they ought to be.

With these things in mind, how then should I view money? Is money evil? Of course not. It is a resource given to us by God to be used and enjoyed. This is where I find myself when I think about the financial resources and material blessings the LORD has so graciously bestowed upon me: attempting to strike the right balance between enjoying the money He gives and not using it unwisely. For to overspend would be foolish, and to underspend would be miserly. If I overspend, I run the risk of getting myself into debt and other similar financial problems. But if I underspend (or overly restrict my financial generosity towards others), I may end up like the man in the Bible who filled his silos full of grain, but whose life that very night God demanded of him. I want to save money, not horde it. Am I being financially foolish? Am I remembering that nothing I have here will go with me to Heaven? Again, there is a balance that must be found.

And so, with all of these thoughts going through my mind, I finally got the inspiration to revisit this idea. "What do we really need?" This is the question I hope to answer in the following poem. Only the title ("Necessities") of the original poem I began writing in Okinawa remains:

A pair of clothes,
That I am not shamed by my nakedness.
A meal to eat,
That my body and mind have strength to achieve.
A glass of water,
That I do not wither and die.
The faithfulness of a companion,
That I have reason to rise when the morning dawns.
The love of a Father,
That I may know my life has meaning and purpose.
The sacrifice of a Savior,

That my transgressions shall not be held against me on
the Day of Judgment.
The Presence of His Spirit,
That I may grow in the knowledge of His truth and love.

For if I have at least these things,
My body will run its course,
And my soul shall live forever.

II

(GRACE BEFORE ETERNITY)

The following is a response I wrote to an essay an acquaintance of mine posted on her blog. The topic of her essay was grace in relation to Luke's account of Jesus's crucifixion, more specifically, the two thieves who were crucified with Jesus that day. Her essay focused on the eternal grace the one thief who accepted Jesus was about to receive as he died and joined Jesus in Paradise. And rightfully so. This particular passage hones in on two men who are on the verge of death, and so, it seems fitting to want to focus on eternity.

However, in our meditations on what we as Christians are promised in eternity, I fear we often lose sight of the fact that God's grace is largely available to us now; we don't have to keep waiting. If the Holy Spirit of the Living God is dwelling inside us and is made one spirit with us here on Earth, then why are we not experiencing the manifestation of His renewing power within us while we are still here on Earth? Sadly, I think it is because there are many Christians who believe that the better part of grace comes only after death, or because they are unwilling to give Jesus the access He needs or to make the sacrifices He requires in order to bring us more completely into His grace.

Experiencing the fullness of God's grace available to us in this life is the topic of my response to her post:

John 10:10 states, "The thief comes only to steal and kill and destroy. I came that they may have life and have it abundantly."

Galatians 5:1 states, "For freedom Christ has set us free; stand firm therefore, and do not submit again to a yoke of slavery."

You wrote a lot about the eternal results of receiving God's grace, but what about the temporal results, the results that we can see in our lives now before we ascend to Heaven to be with Our Father? Are healing and restoration of our hearts and minds available to us only after we have physically died and gone to Heaven?

John (quoting the words of Jesus) and Paul, speak of freedom and abundance. Are freedom and abundance only available to us after we die, or did Jesus die so that we could experience them in the present?

If we have not experienced healing and restoration now in this life, if we are not living in freedom and abundance here on Earth, then what is it that is keeping us from doing so? Is it possible that we ourselves are the problem, that we do not have healing, restoration, freedom, and abundance in our lives now because we are still holding onto things we should be giving over to Jesus? What about our guilt and shame, our fear and pride, the results of our sins and the sins committed against us, the very things Jesus died to eradicate? Do we understand that these things belong on the Holy Cross with Jesus Christ and not in our hearts?

We Christians talk a lot about salvation, and that's good. Because that is one of the reasons Jesus came. But it is not the only reason He came. C.S. Lewis, in his book *The Great Divorce*, talks about both believers and unbelievers and their lives on Earth. He says for the unbeliever, Hell starts now, and that the life they live on Earth is the closest they will ever get to Heaven. However, for the believer, Heaven starts now, and the life they live on Earth is the closest they will ever get to Hell. If after we are saved we do not begin to (increasingly) experience Heaven on Earth, it is because we are not living in the freedom and abundance Jesus the Christ bought for us. And if we are not living in freedom and abundance, it is because we have not allowed Jesus—through the power of the Holy Spirit within us—to do the work in our hearts, minds, and souls necessary to heal us and to restore us.

But if we do allow Him to heal us and to restore us, and we do then live in freedom and abundance, how much more will we be able to bring Heaven to Earth? And if we bring Heaven to Earth in abundance, then how much brighter lights and saltier salts will we be to do the work of salvation in those who are still lost here? Will we not be much more effective Christians and much more effective at carrying out the Great Commission, which is to proclaim the forgiveness of sins through Jesus the Christ alone, and then to make disciples of those who believe?

Healing. Restoration. Freedom. Abundance. These are available to us now. Are we humble enough and willing enough to receive them?

III

(FORTRESS)

When did it begin?
When did you start protecting yourself with lies?
Perhaps you did it to spare someone's feelings.
Or maybe it was to hide your true self,
Afraid to fail or to displease those around you.

She built a fortress of lies around herself
Believing it would offer her protection and refuge.
Brick by brick, stone by stone.
The monstrosity grew with every lie she told.
Now locked in her high tower,
She realizes she forgot to build a gate!

"Who can save me from my fortress!" she cries.
"The fortress I built by my own deeds!
I have kept everything I have ever wanted away from me
    using these walls.
Now I see, the only thing I have kept away is myself.
I have trapped myself in a fortress of my own lies!

Who is strong enough to save me from myself?!
Who is mighty enough to conquer my fortress?!"

I once knew a woman to whom I was willing to give everything I have and everything I am. All she had to do was say yes to us being together, and I would have been hers forever. Or, she could have said no, and I would have respected her wishes and left her alone. But she chose a third option instead: indecision. You see, she wanted me around. She liked what I had to offer, and she liked the *idea* of being with me, but she did not actually want to be with me. She did not want to fully accept me because that meant she would have to give back. She did not want to say yes to us being together because she was unwilling to deal with the ramifications. On the other hand, she did not want to say no either, because she did not want to lose me and the nice feelings I gave her—the euphoria of someone loving you genuinely and passionately. So, rather than make a clear decision about us, she chose instead to keep me at bay with half-truths and indecision, thinking that if she never gave me anything definite, then I would stay in her life indefinitely. And I would have. If it were not for the relational growth and maturity that I experienced as I continued to walk with the LORD, I would have allowed myself to be trapped in her games forever. She intended to keep me around indefinitely, when with a simple "yes," she could have kept me permanently.

Over time, she backed herself deeper and deeper into a corner. I tried to bring the truth of the relationship to light, but every time I did, a new wall was built to defend herself against my advance. One barrier after another she raised between us until it was clear that she had locked herself away in a fortress of her own lies and deceit. She stagnated, and I grew. All the while she continued to call out to me from her high tower in the hope that she would get just a glimmer of the love which she so desperately desired but which she so vehemently refused to accept into her life. Eventually, it became clear to me that the most loving thing to do was, in fact, to leave her to herself and in the Hands of God. In the end, her indecision produced the same result as if she had said no. She got neither me nor my love, and she was left behind, trapped in her fortress with no way out except through humility, confession, and repentance. For when people construct such hardened structures to keep the world around them at what they think is a safe distance, it is the LORD alone who has the power to destroy those walls and free them from themselves.

The behavior this woman displayed toward me: is this not what so many of us do to Jesus? We want His favor, but not Him. We want Him to love us, but we do not want to have to love Him back. We want Him to give us things, but we refuse to give Him anything. We want Him to be around and accessible, but we will not give Him access. We like how He makes us feel, but we do not like Him. We want freedom from pain, sorrow, suffering, and death, but we are unwilling to allow Him to do the work in our lives that is required for us to be free[6] from these. We want Him to save us, but only from our consequences, not our sin. We want to go to Heaven, but only on the condition that He isn't there.

What kind of relationship is this? If someone treated you like this, would you feel inclined to satisfy their requests? Or would you be horribly shocked and offended at such selfishness and utter disregard for the giver of the thing desired? And if we recognize this truth in our human relationships, how then could we possibly expect to receive anything at all from a good and holy God with attitudes like these? We feel entitled to the benefits promised to those who say yes to God, but indecision, lies, and game-playing will produce the same result as flat out rejection of the "free gift of God."[7] And when you find yourself in the place "where the worm never dies, and the fire is not quenched; where there is much

---

[6] When I say "free" I do not mean that once you become a Christian, you will never again experience these things in your time on Earth. But once you accept Jesus into your life, He will begin to heal you and to release you from the pain, sorrow, suffering, and death caused by your sins or the sins committed against you, that is, of course, if you are willing to let Him do the work necessary to accomplish this. And in the life to come, you will be completely free from all of these forever.

[7] Romans 6:23 (ESV)

weeping and gnashing of teeth,"[8] will you have the audacity to blame Him for your condition? Or will you finally, but all too late, realize that He has only ever given you exactly that thing for which you asked, which is to be apart from Him? The Son of Man came into this world to save it, not to condemn it. It is we who condemn ourselves. And because God is both Love and Justice, He will give you what you want.

---

[8] Mark 9:48 (ESV) or Matthew 25:30 (ESV)

IV

(CONSIDER THIS...)

Consider the life of Jesus. Consider the life of Paul. Consider the life of every man or woman mentioned in the Bible who remained faithful to God above all things.

The Christian life is not about how it makes us feel. The Christian life is not about how it makes us feel better about ourselves. The Christian life is about living out God's will and purpose for your life, even when it makes you feel not so great. I have been required to do things that I would rather have not done and that didn't make me feel so good, particularly because they involved people with whom I want to be friends, not enemies; to whom I want to be close, not distant. But as Christians, we must love God and His will more than what we want and more than what others want from us. It is not about us; it is about the God who created us.

The beautiful thing about God, though, is that even while everything is about Him, He is perfectly humble and generously loving, always taking care of us in every way and placing the utmost importance on providing for our every need. He does not leave us behind or forget us. He does not fail us or forsake us. He already knows well enough that everything is about Him; He doesn't need to rub it in our faces. Instead, He offers Himself to us freely and completely as long as we are willing to accept Him and His provision on His terms alone, that is, healthy terms.

Lord God, may those whose hearts need these words find them and receive them well. And may Your Spirit penetrate them to their very soul and spirit. Let their lives be transformed by Your truth, Your love, Your power, and Your mercy. Amen.

V

(FEARING FREEDOM)

"'All things are lawful for me,' but not all things are helpful." 1 Corinthians 6:12 (ESV)

I was reminded yesterday to live free.

I am afraid to totally and completely live in the freedom I have been given because I am afraid that, in the exercising of my freedom, I will one day look up and find that I have wandered off into the desolate wilderness of godlessness and depravity. I am afraid I will forget God. I am afraid I will displease or dishonor Him. I am afraid to be wrong or to make mistakes. Fear oppresses, and it leads to self-suppression and an inability to simply do and enjoy the many things in this life which bring me great pleasure, even though most of these have nothing to do with morality, or with sin versus righteousness. Ultimately, I am afraid of myself. I know the darkness in my heart, and I know the evil—the terrible, horrible evil—of which I am capable. I realize I am no better than

King David or Samson. And though, in the end, these were declared righteous and faithful by God, I do not wish to follow in their footsteps.

I am reminded to live free and without fear.

"There is no fear in love, but perfect love casts out fear. For fear has to do with punishment, and whoever fears has not been perfected in love." 1 John 4:18 (ESV)

VI

(GOING HOME)

Before I knew Christ,
I would stay up late,
Watching things I should not have been watching,
Doing things I should not have been doing.
Emptiness consumed my soul.
Hopelessness plagued my heart.
Meaninglessness tortured my mind.

"There has to be more to life than this!
There has to be something greater for which to live!
Pleasure has lost its pleasure,
Enjoyment brings me no joy,
And life itself feels like death!"

Death…
It was constantly in my thoughts.
If there is nothing beyond this,
If there is nothing for which to hope,
Then it matters not whether I live or die.

Death…
It was constantly on my mind.

But He gave me hope.
He gave me purpose.
He gave me meaning.
He showed me that there is something beyond this;
There is something for which to hope.
Nothing I do in His Name will go unnoticed,
Nor will it be forgotten,
Nor will it fade and dissolve into the infinitude of history.
For He knows me by name,
And He knows my comings and goings,
And He knows the words I speak,
And the things I do,
And the thoughts upon which I dwell.
And He Himself has said,
"I go to prepare a place for you in my Father's house."

Death…
The thought still lingers.
But now for a different reason:
I long for death,
That my soul could be released from my flesh.
I long for death,
That I may see Him and the things He has prepared with
    my own eyes.
I long for death,
That I may finally know peace and rest.

I long for death,
That I may finally go Home.

I want to go Home…

What do you do when all you can think about is how much you want to die? Not because you are suicidal, but because you long to be released from the constant struggle of this life. How do you react to this? How do you continue on in obedience for a lifetime when you feel as though you won't even make it through today?

I think about the fact that I could very well live—LORD willing—another 50, 60, maybe even 70 years. And sometimes, quite frankly, that really doesn't sound all that appealing. Even for those of us who live in a "nice" country or a "good" country like the United States, life is still filled with struggle, anguish, anxiety, stress, pain, death, sorrow, suffering, injustice, corruption, greed, poverty, starvation, rape, murder, abuse, hate, evil, and sin. There is not a place in this life, on this planet, or anywhere in the entirety of the physical universe where one can go to find real peace or true rest. That's kind of depressing, yeah? But at the same time, for the believer, it actually draws you closer to His throne because the awful crap that happens in this world makes you appreciate even more how contrary to this world Our King really is. "I am not of this world," Jesus tells us in John 8:23 (ESV). Thank God He is not. The last thing I want when

I regain consciousness in Heaven is to awaken to another world just like this one.

But the Kingdom of Heaven is quite different. Read The Beatitudes from The Sermon on the Mount in Matthew 5:1-12. Then flip to Revelation 21:1-8. From these passages, we see that in God's Kingdom, there is no pain. There is no death. There is no thirst or hunger. There is no discomfort, no prideful or arrogant people who hurt others in order to raise themselves up. There are no tears, or crying, or mourning, or nights filled with sorrow. There are no funerals, no betrayal, or murder, or corruption. There are no rejections, no slanderous words spoken against us, no persecution, no injustice, no unwarranted hatred aimed at us.

For the time being, however, we are expatriates, exiled, in a sense, from our Home, painfully longing to return to our native land of righteousness and perfection. How then do you continue on in obedience during the times when all you want is for God to strike you dead where you stand? When all you want is for Him to put you into a deep sleep and take the breath from your lungs? You start by confessing these thoughts and feelings to Him with every emotion attached to them. You confess them, not because it is sin to feel this way, but because Your Father cares deeply for you and your struggles. He wants to help you, He wants to hear from you, and He wants to comfort you like only He can when the pain goes so deep it becomes existential.

You learn to be content with where He places you in life. You learn to be satisfied with the answers He gives to your prayers and your deepest desires, especially the "no's" and "not yet's." You learn to love Him and His will so much that you refuse to take your life into your own hands. You learn to keep your faith, hope, and love firmly rooted in the person of Jesus Christ.

You remember that nothing you do here in His Name goes unnoticed or unrewarded. You remember that this world and the life you live in it are only temporary. If God did not have a reason for you to still be here, then you would not still be here. And, perhaps most importantly, you remember that His Kingdom exists not just in Heaven, but also in your heart and in your spirit; His Kingdom is with you and in you always. For the Holy Spirit of the Living God dwells within you. You are His Kingdom, and He will bring you Home.

VII

(HYPOCRITE)

Did David write one of his psalms the night before
He adultered the wife and murdered her husband?
Did Paul write his second letter to the Corinthians
The day after the thorn tormented him again?
At what point did Peter forgive himself enough to preach
The Name of his Friend and Savior,
The very Man he denied three times as the rooster
    crowed?

Sometimes I feel like such a hypocrite,
When my left hand honors Him,
And my right hand curses His Name,
When my mind, heart, and mouth sing His praises,
And my body blasphemes Him.

Forgive me, Father, and discipline me,
That I may follow you!
For even now,
The sins of my past lurk in the shadows of my mind.

My sin grieves me.
I am appalled at the thoughts and intentions of a so-
called "man of God."
After years of walking closely with My Lord,
Still this filth crawls and creeps forth from the lingering
darkness in my heart.
It is a disease.
It tries to plague me once more.

Will I ever be free?
Will I ever be able to live and walk in complete
Righteousness and purity?
Will my thoughts, words, and deeds ever be perfectly
consistent?
I feel so dirty, but I know I am cleansed.
I feel so guilty and ashamed, but I know I am forgiven.
I am a citizen in The Kingdom, but still so far from
home.
Lead me not into temptation, LORD,
But deliver me from the evil that begins in myself.

When you really think about it, there is an extraordinary amount of hypocrisy involved in human interaction. "Please stop smacking your lips while you're eating. It's annoying." I have done annoying things too. "That guy is driving way too fast." I drive over the speed limit all the time. "You shouldn't be sleeping with your friend's wife (or husband)." Many times have I lusted after a woman who is not my wife, and this meets Jesus's definition of adultery in Matthew 5:27-28. And these are only a few examples. So you see, there is a great deal of hypocrisy between us humans. We are constantly telling others not to do things we ourselves do or have done. Realizing this, it would be very easy to be overcome by a sense of social paralysis, a sense that we cannot say anything to anyone no matter what they are doing because, at the end of the day, we have *all* broken every one of God's laws and commandments at some point in time.

But there are several places in the Bible where the writer actually encourages us to confront others about their sin and to use Scripture to help the brother or sister confronted to see the error of their ways. So how then do we confront others about their sin when we still have so much sin in our own lives?

1) We condemn the behavior, not the person. It is not man's job to condemn other men to "the eternal fire prepared for the devil and his angels."[9] That is God's job. It is within His authority alone to judge us. Furthermore, it is his right to judge us since He alone is sinless and without hypocrisy, and it is He against whom we have sinned. It is, however, biblically within our authority as brothers and sisters in Christ to lovingly point out a pattern or a lifestyle of impure or unrighteous behavior in another believer: first as an individual, then with one

---

[9] Matthew 25:41 (ESV)

or two witnesses, and finally as a church. Jesus said if we love Him, we will keep his commandments. God has spoken to us and has explained to us what his standard is. In light of these things, we cannot simply go about living our lives as we please. But at the same time, it is of no use to try and point out every sin and every time someone screws up. That would be extremely tiresome and overwhelmingly irritating. Therefore, if you do feel it necessary to confront a brother or sister about their behavior, pray about it first and be sure that it is something worth the confrontation. Asking a third party's opinion or even asking them to help you with the confrontation is always a good idea as well. LORD, please give us wisdom and discernment, truth and love.

2) We remember that, as Christians, we do not preach perfection based on our own ability, but that Jesus is perfection for us. We humbly admit before the LORD that we have been guilty there as well. As I stated previously, we have all violated every single one of God's commandments at one point or another. (Yes, you have. Take a moment to truly consider this in the context of God's Law and the complementary teachings of Jesus, and it won't take long for you to see this.) "For all have sinned and fall short of the Glory of God." These are Paul's words in Romans 3:23 (ESV). When we recognize, acknowledge, and confess that we are also guilty, then we avoid hypocrisy and instead are able to confront others

from a stance of humility and love. God is pleased by this, and He is able to use it to great effect.

3) We encourage others to pursue righteousness out of love and a sincere desire to see them grow, while being sure to leave plenty of room for grace, patience, and forgiveness the same way God does for us. After all, in everyone's pursuit of holy behavior, there are bound to be plenty of slip-ups. God understands this, and so should we.

"Finally, all of you, have unity of mind, sympathy, brotherly love, a tender heart, and a humble mind." 1 Peter 3:8 (ESV)

"Love one another with brotherly affection. Outdo one another in showing honor." Romans 12:10 (ESV)

If you truly love someone, you will want to see them grow, improve, and become the best version of themselves that they can possibly be. This includes telling people the truth, even when you know it may hurt them in the moment, because you see that the long term effects will be beneficial. Is this not the same reason we discipline and/or spank our children?

"Wounds from a sincere friend are better than many kisses from an enemy." Proverbs 27:6 (NLT)

This does not mean you must say everything that is true; not all "wounds" are necessary to inflict, nor are they always yours to inflict. But it does mean that the things you do say should be true. God is Truth, and God is Love. He is not either/or, and He is not more one than the other depending on the occasion. He is both. At all times.

VIII

(NOW, AND NOT YET): Reflections on the dichotomy of my existence

Spirit and Flesh

My existence is dichotomous. I am a soul made of spiritual essence which has, possesses, inhabits a body made of physical matter. My spirit and my flesh.

These were once in unison. I felt no struggle because my soul, under the condemnation of God's Justice, agreed with my flesh and freely and without hindrance pursued the temporal pleasures of a rotting and decaying world. My mind and my heart were being trained in the ways of destruction. Evil and depravity infected my soul. Great damage was done to the Image I was made to bear. It must be undone. My condition was an eternal flat line. I must be revived. I must be re-taught how to walk in the ways of My Father. I must rediscover the obedience and the submission which my soul forgot ages ago in a

Garden. Who will help me do this? Who will place the paddles to my chest? Who will rescue me from the depths of Sheol? Who but My King, My Lover, My Friend?

Alliances are broken. Companions become bitter rivals. A great struggle ensues. A war unseen rages inside me. My spirit, connected to a good and holy God, desires life, freedom, faith, hope, and love. My flesh, trapped in a physical realm corrupted by sin, craves death, greed, hate, slavery, and perversion. The flesh must die. It does not deserve to live. This is my existence. I am a walking, living, breathing paradox.

Internal and External

There is an internal (personal) aspect to my dichotomy, an aspect which only My King and I truly know. Though my external deeds may more often reflect the new desires of my heart as I am conformed to the Image of the Son, internally, in the lingering shadows of my heart and mind, my old nature lurks and creeps. It seeks opportunities to feed itself on my sin that it may grow stronger and re-infest a heart that has been purified by the Blood of the Lamb. My thoughts can be quite perverted, and my intentions rather ignoble, even if the ultimate result which other people see from me is actions that are pleasing to the Father.

But My King was flawless in thought, word, and deed. And so I must strive for this ideal. His aim is the transformation of my heart and the renewing of my mind. In this way, my intentions will properly reflect His divine character, and from proper intentions come proper actions. My actions will become the outpouring of the love and grace I experienced the day I accepted The Sacrifice. The flesh will be severely disciplined and made subservient to my spirit. For it is my soul which contains my consciousness and my will, and it is my spirit which is reconnected to and invited to rejoin in the Holy Communion of the Trinity by the impartation of the Holy Spirit. He binds me to Him. He makes us one. I am made in His Image. He longs for me to be like Him, and He desires that I should properly reflect His glory.

My body will enter the tomb and return to the dust from which it came. But my soul will be resurrected with The Lamb and be brought into new life. My flesh is dying all around my living spirit, but they are now still together for a time. It is clear that my body must perish if I am to meet perfection.

The Reconciliation

I am perfect in His Sight. Yet my life is filled with imperfections. How do I manage this? How do I reconcile my desire to please Him with my daily failures to live up to His standards and expectations? Grace.

Grace is forgiveness. Grace is mercy. Grace is having sympathy and, because of the Christ, empathy on my condition. Grace is the freedom to enjoy Him. Grace is offering a bastard child of sin a place in the Father's house. Grace is utterly destroying His Son so that His Eyes may look upon me as if I were the Son. Except that His love for me says so, I do not deserve this grace. That is why it is called grace. It is a pardon for my transgressions. It is a cancellation of my iniquities. It is the payment of an outrageous debt. It is the restoration of the Image I bear. It is the renovation of a collapsing heart and mind. It is the rejuvenation of a condemned soul. It is the liberty to make mistakes without the fear of reprisal or judgment. It is the assurance of things promised. It is the reward of faith. Grace is the reconciliation of a soul made perfect by The Blood which must coexist (for a time) with a body doomed to the grave for its imperfections.

His grace makes me perfect now, and also not yet.

IX

(公民/CITIZENSHIP)

旅游时,
本地人说: 你是美国人。
但回答: 没什么公民。
他们说: 你住在世界上。
可回答: 我家这里不在。
对我说: 你是活人。
不过回: 我已经死了。
我的道理他们不懂。
告诉他们: 多了解父亲。

When I travel,
The locals say: "You are an American."
But I reply: "I have no citizenship."
They say: "You live in this world."
But I answer: "My home is not here."
They say to me: "You are a living human being."
But I respond: "I am already dead."
They do not understand my logic.
I tell them: "Seek to know the Father."

I was physically born in the United States of America in 1988. I have a birth certificate and a social security card from the same. At one point, I had two passports, one tourist and one official, as well as a driver's license from California and an active duty military ID card. There is no mistaking who I am or in what country the LORD planted me. But is my citizenship really in America? Or am I an ambassador of a greater nation? Certainly I have taken up residency in this country. But is not my home yet many decades away in a distant, hidden Kingdom? Is this Kingdom of which I speak even hidden, or is it so obvious that people are blind to its existence? Can anyone truly be blind to its existence, or only willfully ignorant of their place in it?

Hebrews 11:13-16 (ESV) reads: "These all died in faith, not having received the things promised, but having seen them and greeted them from afar, and having acknowledged that they were strangers and exiles on the earth. For people who speak thus make it clear that they are seeking a homeland. If they had been thinking of that land from which they had gone out, they would have had opportunity to return. But as it is, they desire a better country, a heavenly one. Therefore God is not ashamed to be called their God, for he has prepared for them a city."

I no longer seek a homeland, for I know He has prepared one for me in advance. I no longer wish to establish myself in this country, because I understand that I am here only on a work visa. I no longer strive to promote the democracy within these man-made boundaries, because it is clear that I represent a Theocracy that is without borders. I no longer attempt to preserve my life, for truly death is the only transportation capable of delivering me safely to my destination. I simply desire to finish well my life here, that I may begin forever my life there.

X

(I SAW HER PASSING AMONGST THE TREES)

What fault can I find in her character?
What flaw can I find in her beauty?
None! For there is none of which to speak!
Her presence is like a radiant light.
Her touch soft and delicate like the morning dew.
She moves with grace and humility like a doe through
the forest.
Purity and righteousness are the garments she wears.
Adorned with the Presence of the LORD,
She is a daughter of the Most High.

When I wrote this poem, I envisioned myself standing in the middle of a lush, green forest with beams of sunlight descending through the canopy and gently landing upon the rocks, the shrubs, and the grasses below. The forest is peaceful and still. It is quiet and calm. A typical outdoor experience, the only wildlife that is readily apparent are the birds which play and hop amongst the branches. But even these are not always visible. They make their presence known not by exposing themselves to my observation, but by diligently singing their favorite Divinely-inspired songs. Perhaps a few butterflies here and there. They have always seemed so awkward to me. Their airborne style appears to be more like a series of controlled falls rather than actual flight, with their rapid changes in elevation as they bob and float silently amid the streams of sunlight.

At this point, I could add some fluffiness to the image by bringing in a few deer or rabbits, but I honestly haven't seen all that many creatures beyond bugs and birds in most of my outdoor adventures. I have seen a great deal of antelope driving through the middle north of the United States. And I have seen a significant number of fish, but those are always stuck to my fishing hook. Plus, there's no stream in this part of the forest. I don't know. Maybe I've been hanging out in the wrong forests. Like I said, this is a typical outdoor experience, not an animated Disney movie.

Anyway, matching the tranquility of the forest, I stand amidst the greenery and vegetation peacefully enjoying that which His Hands have made. Life, both seen and unseen, flourishes around me and continues on with total disregard for my presence. I am inconsequential to this place.

Movement in my peripheral, and my attention shifts to the most beautiful woman I have ever seen. She moves into the open as if birthed by the trees of the forest themselves. As she steps forward, her gown of purest white flows from her body as if it were leaving behind a trail of her essence. I stand there, staring intently, begging my mind to conceive a word or a thought to describe the vision before me. She doesn't see me, and then she does. Our eyes find each other, and in a moment, I am inspired with a description fitting of such an excellent woman of God.

Read Proverbs 31:10-31 from whichever translation of the Holy Scriptures tickles your fancy the most.

We often like to tell little girls when they are young, "You're a princess," or, "You're so precious," or, "You are such a beautiful little treasure," and other such things. These things are true. A woman is meant to be the beauty of the Living God made manifest in human form. And Proverbs 18:22 states: "He who finds a wife finds a treasure, and receives favor from the LORD." But let us not forget that the beauty of Our Lord is found much more in His character than in His appearance. After all, we cannot see the Living God. And Isaiah 53 tells us that Jesus was a man of unremarkable appearance. My point here is not that physical beauty should be disregarded. I myself am a man who very much appreciates a woman with a graceful figure and a pretty face. However, if her beauty stops at her physical attributes, and there is nothing else to go along with it, then this is not a woman whose beauty is perfected in Christ. This is not a woman who understands that her beauty starts with things unseen—namely the character of a good and Holy God being fostered within her heart and her mind—and then is made complete by what is seen.

What is my point then? It is that simply being born a woman does not make you a "precious jewel." Proverbs 31 says a virtuous, or an excellent, or a capable wife is more precious than fine rubies, not just a wife. Assuming a woman is a precious jewel by virtue of her being a woman and nothing else is similar to assuming a car is a quality car worthy of adoration just because it's a car. But clearly we can see that some cars are of a superior quality over others. Japanese cars are known for their reliability. German cars are known for their engineering and performance. So we see that simply because something is what it is, its existence alone as such should not result in praise or admiration. I do not admire a painting because it is a painting, but because it is a well done painting, and I can admire it as such even if I do not necessarily like the painting itself. That is to say, I can admire the beauty of a woman's character even if I do not connect with her personality because character is objective while personality is not. And it is the quality of a woman's character which makes her a precious jewel, not her physical beauty or her gender.

I have personally encountered much pride and discontentment towards men amongst the female race due to this simple misunderstanding of what makes a woman truly valuable and precious. Although *all* people, both male and female, should be treated with kindness, dignity, and respect (even when they are undeserving), there are too many women in this world that think they somehow deserve something extra just because they are a woman. Extra attention, or extra love, or extra special treatment. It is like a sense of entitlement, as if being born a woman (which, by the way, you had no control over) automatically qualifies you for something above and beyond others. But a woman is not more valuable than other people because she is a woman. And a beautiful woman is not more valuable than other women because she is blessed with more physical beauty than they. Nor is it proper for a woman to use other men's ill-treatment of her to justify her demands of special consideration or her reciprocated ill-treatment of men. But a woman increases her value beyond her inherent human value by more closely reflecting the Image of the One by whom she was created. And a great deal of His character is Humility.

Men, this passage applies to you as well. In Ephesians 5, Paul calls the Church "the bride of Christ" of which men are a part. Therefore, in your relationship with Jesus, men, you play the female role. You are the bride, and Jesus is the groom. You are the woman, and Jesus is the man. I know reading this will probably make a lot of you men who have a strong sense of masculinity cringe, but it is true. And just like it takes a great deal of humility for a wife to submit to the leadership of her husband (especially if the husband is not a particularly excellent leader), so also we men must be humble and accept our role as the wife in relation to Jesus by submitting to His leadership and authority over us. If you as a man are not humble enough to accept this, then you surely should not expect your wife to humble herself for you. A leader who is worth following humbly sacrifices his life for those whom he loves and leads. If you do not believe me, then read Matthew 20:25-28 or Mark 10:42-45. Be a man worth following. Be a man worthy of your wife's submission. Be a good wife yourself.

And lastly, somewhat off topic but still related to the preceding discussion, I will close by saying that there are a great many people who are missing significant portions of His character in their lives because they have labeled that portion either "male" or female," rather than labeling it "God." As followers and disciples of Jesus the Christ, we should desire to reflect the fullness of God's character, not just the "male" or "female" parts of it.

XI

(LETTER TO A FRIEND)
& (FAITHFUL)

The following is a letter I wrote to a friend of mine. The goal of this letter was to share a part of my life with her—to share a portion of my testimony relevant to our discussion in the hope that it would encourage her to surrender this part of her life to Jesus so that she could receive His healing and restoration. And, for the sake of being completely honest, as it will be apparent in the content of the letter, I was also hoping that once she had received Jesus into this part of her life, she and I could share a relationship together.

You know, it's interesting, my friend. Not more than two years ago, I wouldn't have even considered pursuing a woman as beautiful as you are. My heart and mind were too full of pride and lies about myself and about God to even consider the possibility of being with the kind of woman I truly desire. I would get bitter and hateful toward myself, toward God, and toward women. I would say things to myself like, "SEE! You're ugly and unattractive! And women DESPISE you! You're undesirable! That's why women don't want to be with you! That's why you'll NEVER get married, NEVER have a family, NEVER be with a woman in intimacy!.....SEE! God doesn't WANT to provide you with a wife! And even if he did, He COULDN'T! Because women hate you anyway!" It was so bad that even when women did take notice of me, I would refuse to entertain the possibility. I would refuse to allow myself to even conceive something so preposterous. And then I would drown my sorrows and self-pity in all kinds of pornography and sexual perversion to numb the pain of the hope that was trying to take hold inside me, but which I refused to allow or accept. I refused to allow it because, at the time, in my heart of hearts (or at least temporarily in those moments), I truly believed that a computer screen was as close to a beautiful woman as I would ever get. It was terrible, and it was evil, and it was dark, and it was straight from the pit of Hell and the mouth of Satan. And when I was done medicating myself, the shame and guilt of what I had forced into my mind—all those perverted images that were now seared into my memory—would be overwhelming. I would fall onto the floor before God begging Him to forgive me and to cleanse me and to heal me of this prideful disease and to repair the damage that I was doing to myself, to my relationship with Him, and to the relationship with my future wife.

I was exposed to pornography when I was about nine or ten years old. I committed my life to Jesus when I was 13. Not until I was 25, however, was the LORD finally able to bring me to a place where that pride and those lies in my heart—even more so that pride and those lies which I had made a part of my very soul—could be crushed and defeated and removed from me forever. I remember the feeling well.

I was lying in bed, wrestling with my thoughts about all the rejections I had faced up to that point, wrestling with my thoughts about pornography and how much I hated it, but also how much I was still drawn to it. And I remember the LORD saying to me, "Are you ready?" My pitiful reply, as a child who knows the doctor is about to cause him pain in order to make him better, "Uh-huh." The lights were off. My eyes were closed. I covered my face with my pillow. And still somehow things around me became darker. I began to feel a pressure in my chest. But not in my physical chest. If my soul has a chest, that's where the pressure was. And the pressure steadily increased over the course of just a few seconds until it felt as if a part of my very existence was being crushed inside me. I was being executed, my friend. The lies and the pride within me were being spiritually executed, and the feeling that resulted was one of deep spiritual agony and anguish. I've never felt anything like it. The only thing I can think of that might compare is how it must feel to die. At its height, I gave a loud cry into the pillow that covered my face.

And then...it was gone! As quickly as its onset, so was its departure. And the PEACE, my friend!!! The Peace I felt when He was done, it was unlike anything I had ever experienced or am likely to experience until I see Him face-to-face. I felt as though I was rising from the grave into a NEW new life. I had already received Him as my Lord and Savior: new life number one. But now He was raising me a second time, a second new life, a new life uncorrupted by pride, lies, guilt, shame, doubt, or fear. Still tied to my physical body, and therefore still imperfect and sinful, but internally, in my spirit, so cleansed, so renewed, so FREE! And this is why I am able to see what is true so clearly now. I could see truth before, but it was always muddied up with the untruth and the lies I was still harboring inside, and because of this, it made it much more difficult for me to be certain about God and myself and many things in life that are now so plainly apparent to me.

Why am I telling you all this? Because I see that you, my friend, still have a great deal of guilt, shame, and pride in your own life because of the decisions you have made and because of the way other men, namely the father of your son, have treated you. And I want you to know, my friend, that Your God values you, and He loves you, and He places a tremendous amount of worth upon you and your life. If this weren't true, then why would He send Jesus, His own Son, to die for you? No one sacrifices their one and only son for someone they do not value or do not place the most incredible amount of worth upon. And I'm telling you that if you are humble enough and willing enough to allow Jesus to do the work and the deed in your life that He has done in mine, then you too can experience a whole other level of His truth and His love that I now experience daily.

You say that you're not interested in me and that you don't put a very high priority on dating and relationships right now. I don't believe this is true, but I will take your word for it, my friend. However, regardless of your interest in me or any other man, I will tell you this, and I tell you this not out of condemnation or accusation as Satan would do, but out of love and a desire for you to experience what I have and continue to experience with My Lord: you will *never* get what you truly desire out of yourself, out of your life, out of your husband, or out of Your God if you are unwilling to put aside your pride and let Jesus deal with your guilt and shame in the manner in which it needs to be dealt. This I know is true, and it is directly from the Mouth of the Father. Amen.

I will close this letter with a poem I hope to share with my wife someday. I wrote this back in November of 2012 as a reflection of the work the LORD was/is doing in my life in preparation to receive one of His daughters as my bride. I share it with you now simply as something that may give you a further glimpse into the man the LORD is raising me up to be.

(FAITHFUL)

I love my wife dearly,
And I don't even know who she is.
I miss her,
But know not how it feels to be in her presence.
I long for her,
But have yet to touch her skin or hear her voice.
I am one with her,
But from her still separated by an unknown distance.
I am waiting for her,
But she is already with me now.
I am a faithful, loving husband,
Yet my finger wears no gold.

Being with you would not be a waste of who I am and who the LORD has raised me up to be, my friend.

In Christ, Christ in me
Peter G

XII

(MY DESIRE BURNS FOR YOU)

My desire, Beloved, it burns for you.
Inside me, a raging furnace consumes my soul.
My thoughts are set ablaze with passion when I think
    of you.
Day and night I pray for you,
I long for you,
I yearn for you,
I beg My Father in Heaven to provide you.
I am waiting for you to arrive, My Queen,
That I may make you mine.
I am waiting for His provision, My Bride,
That I may give myself utterly to you.
Yes, I will sacrifice everything I have,
Everything I own,
Everything I have ever wanted;
My hopes, my dreams,
My plans for the future mean nothing to me
If only I could see your face and hear your voice,

If only I could feel your embrace and touch your skin.

My God, is it wrong that I desire this so incredibly?
Is it wrong that my wife consumes so many of my
  thoughts,
So much of my prayers to You?
Should I not first desire You like this, My King?
But I do.
But you are already mine,
And I am already Yours.

How can someone unknown mean so much to me?
How can someone faceless be so desirable to me?
How can I love someone nameless so greatly?

My desire, Oh, My Beloved,
It burns for you like the surface of the sun upon my
  skin…
And still…I wait for you.

I sit in my apartment with one thing on my mind: to
be united with a woman whom I have never met. She
is My Queen. She is My Treasure. She is My "Favor
from the LORD."[10] She is My Prized Possession. She
is My "Precious Jewel."[11] She is My Ephesians 5. She is
My Proverbs 31. She is My 1 Corinthians 13. She is My
Sacrifice. She is My Companion. She is My Friend. She is

---

[10] Proverbs 18:22 (ESV)
[11] Proverbs 31:10 (ESV)

My "Pearl of Great Value."[12] She is My "Treasure Hidden in a Field."[13] She is My Rib. She is My Body. She is My Bride. She is My Church.

I can see her in my dreams. I have visions of her day and night. I know how it feels to be in her presence, yet I have never met her. She is in my mind. She is in my heart. She is in my prayers constantly as I beg My Father to remove her from my mind and make her into reality. I know her well, but I do not know her name. She is so close I can feel her in my arms returning my embrace. And yet how far she is from me now, I know not. If my desire for her were manifested, it would be a raging fire that would consume cities to uncover her.

To touch her skin would overwhelm my existence. To hear her voice call out to me would send me soaring into the highest heavens. To watch her move would bring me to my knees. To simply know her name would fill my heart with the utmost gratitude. A name, LORD, even just a name!

Refine me in your fire, O, LORD. Purify my heart and my mind. Bring my love and passion to an intense, glowing heat, focused and determined to raise My Bride up to you holy and blameless, without spot or wrinkle.[14] Make

---

[12] Matthew 13:45,46 (ESV)

[13] Matthew 13:44 (ESV)

[14] Ephesians 5:27

me worthy of receiving such a blessing. Make me worthy of the woman I have seen in my dreams, the woman I have read about in Your Word.

Beloved, I wait for you. I am saving myself for you. And when the blessed day comes that I may look into your eyes, I will declare to you that no other shall have my strength, that no other shall have my desire, that no other shall have my love. For "I am my beloved's, and my beloved is mine."[15]

...I am waiting for you.

Come...let us be one.

---

[15] Song of Solomon 6:3 (ESV)

XIII

(MY KING, MY LOVER, MY FRIEND)

The Sovereign of Nations rules the nation of my heart and mind with absolute control. His dominion and authority over my life is complete. There is not one span of my body or soul that He does not own. In the throne room of my heart, He is seated with prominence, with eminence above all other desires. A great conqueror, He invaded my life with His love and light. He called me into His service out of the darkness of despair and utter misery. And now, He leads me into battle; He leads me with righteousness and truth into the War of Ages. He is benevolent and kind. He is firm and just. He reigns over my existence as a father looks over the life of his son and raises him in the ways of authentic manhood. He is eternal royalty. His bloodline descends into infinite ages. His dynasty is everlasting. He is My King.

My Husband loves me with the utmost humility and sacrifice. He gave His Life that I may be delivered to Himself without spot or wrinkle, without blemish or impurity.[16] He imparted His Spirit unto me making us one in spirit, just as a man and his wife are one flesh. He is full of forgiveness and mercy when I fail. He is kind and comforting when I fall. He encourages me and uplifts my spirit when I despair. He is always faithful, never leaving me or divorcing me or banishing me from His Presence, even when I do my best to give Him every reason and just cause for doing so. When I am unfaithful, He remains. When I curse His Name, He rebukes me with loving kindness. When I commit adultery against Him,[17] He is quick to forgive and counts it not against me. When I break my vows to Him, He renews our marital covenant. When I defile our marriage bed, He cleanses it with His own Blood. He is My Lover.

Where can I go that My Dearest Companion will not also be? If I go down to the grave, He has been there already to shut its mouth. If I ascend to the heavens, He is there, for it is His dwelling place. If I wrap myself in darkness, His light shines through me. If I stand on the surface of the sun, His glory is brighter still.[18] Every

---

[16] Ephesians 5:27

[17] Throughout the Bible, especially in the books of the Prophets, God makes sin synonymous with adultery as it is a violation of the "spiritual marriage" between God and man.

[18] Psalm 139:7-12

thought in my mind, every word from my mouth, every action I take, He knows and understands completely; He knows me better than I know myself. My darkest secrets, my most horrific sins, the things no one else sees are plain to Him. And yet, His love and loyalty are constant. Willingly, He lays down His life on my behalf. No one takes it from Him, but He gives it freely[19] for He sees the need of my condition. I am never alone or without an ear to listen. My hopes and dreams He delights in. My fears and insecurities He replaces with boldness and confidence founded on His everlasting love and His unshakable truth. He will neither fail me nor forsake me. He is with me always, even to the end of the age.[20] He is My Friend.

---

[19] John 10:18
[20] Matthew 28:20

XIV

(POWER)

He crushes the planets with His bare Hands,
And He brings the rain to water the lands.
With a thought of His Mind, the stars explode.
On the greatest and the worst day,
Unfailing love He showed.
He knits together bones and sinew.
His vision penetrates; He sees all the way in you.
Light and dark are the same to Him.
In His heavenly dwelling,
He is worshiped and adored by holy seraphim.
Infinite wonder and majestic power,
His origin could never be traced back to a single hour.
A God of love and mercy and justice and truth;
The mysteries of His ways are hidden,
Even from the most cunning sleuth.
Night to day, death to life.
His Word is living and active,
Dividing soul and spirit as a knife.

O, pitiful man, where is your power now?
For The King is coming,
And every knee will bow.

Man thinks he has power. He kills and destroys to build
his insignificant kingdom, and he thinks he has power.
Animals kill other animals—and even humans on
occasion—out of fear, instinct, necessity, or curiosity. A
drunk driver in his stupor wanders into oncoming traffic
and destroys lives, families, vehicles, and infrastructure
without even realizing it. Is the power to kill and to
destroy really all that impressive or uncommon?

So what is real power, O, man? Are death and
carnage—whether they be physical, mental, emotional,
or spiritual—the real standard and measure of one's
authority? Can we gauge the quality of a king by the
beauty of his palace? Does the number of Bentleys you
own give you control over the wind and waves? Is your
bank account big enough to buy the stars in the galaxy?
Will the size of your entourage save you from the power
of death? Do you have the power of life and love to
resurrect your dying marriage? Can you pass enough
laws and ordinances to regulate the hearts of men?

Real power builds and creates. Real power upholds and
sustains. Real power breathes Life into dying flesh and
raises it from the grave. Real power loves the unlovable.
Real power shows patience and kindness to the stubborn

and prideful. Real power draws you in and captures your gaze with beauty. Real power whispers to your heart, calling you to return home.

I know not of any mortal man who possesses a single one of these. Because real power belongs to God alone.

XV

(THE PAIN OF HOPE)

I once read an explanation of hope (C.S. Lewis I think) which described it as being so difficult because it is the desire for that which is not yet present or possessed. We can see the thing in our minds, and we can feel it in our hearts. We can have wonderful visions and beautiful dreams exploring what this thing may be like once we have it, but we do not yet have it. And so, instead, it burns and aches inside our soul, even to the point of causing, in a sense, a deep feeling of loss or pain.

One would think that the thing for which I hope that causes this spiritual phenomenon is God and Heaven. Certainly, on occasion, this is true. But I know in my heart that Jesus and Heaven are already mine to keep; He has given, and I have received. Instead, I find that thing for which I hope which causes this burning and aching most often is my desire to find—or perhaps a better word is receive—a wife. I long for and yearn to be an excellent husband to my bride and father to my children, full of unfailing love and unwavering truth; to be one flesh with my beloved and to bestow upon her my life, my love, and myself. Mutual possession: she will have my strength, and I will have her beauty. This is my passion. This is my desire. This is my hope for the future of my life on Earth.

Too often I have tried to numb the pain caused by hope with counterfeits and knock-offs. It is time I learn how to embrace and abide in hope. Lord Jesus, I pray and ask that You would teach me how to bear the pain of hope. Amen.

XVI

(TROUBLED BY DEATH):
Reflections on John 11:28-37

Why do we mourn death so intensely if we believe in a God who is Life?

If we believe in a God who is Mercy and Goodness and Justice, why do we mourn over those who have gone to see Him? Should we not rather mourn for those of us who remain here, for those of us who remain, as Paul wrote, "in the flesh?" In 1 Corinthians 15:50 (ESV), Paul writes "flesh and blood cannot inherit the Kingdom of God." With this in mind, and for those who have received His forgiveness, should we not instead rejoice over those who are no longer flesh and blood? And from this perspective, when we mourn, are we not actually mourning because we have lost, not because they have died? And if we mourn because of our loss while forgetting about their gain, can it not be said that mourning then becomes a selfish, self-centered[21] engagement, and that, in a way, it shows a lack of trust and confidence in God's power and in His promises? Does God not have more right to His children than we do? I feel it much more appropriate to mourn for us, those who remain on the battlefield, rather than for those whose Earthly missions[22] are complete.

In John 11, Jesus did not weep over Lazarus. Lazarus was just fine. Jesus wept because it hurt Him to see those whom He loved hurting. Now, please do not take this to mean I think it is wrong to be sad over the death of a loved one. That is *not* what I am saying. Nor am I saying that death is good. God is Life, which means that death is the opposite of God and is, therefore, bad. But what about life after death? From what I hear, life after death is significantly more desirable than life before it. Unfortunately, apart from rapture, physical death is the only way we can get to life after death. Death is a sad reality, and it is one of the many ways our sin has made things not the way they are supposed to be. God Himself is deeply troubled by death, and this is why the Son of Man tasted death on our behalves. However, before He

---

[21] When I say "selfish" and "self-centered", I do not necessarily mean to attach to these words the strong negative connotation they normally possess. I simply use them as adjectives describing an attitude, mindset, or perspective that is more focused on oneself than maybe it ought to be.

[22] I use the word "missions" in both the military sense and in the sense of missionary work.

did taste death, the Son of Man explained to us that He is "the resurrection and the life."[23] And then he proved it, multiple times, not only by raising others from the dead, but, most importantly, by raising Himself.[24] Therefore, in our mourning, should we not also find hope in the One who is Life and be encouraged by what He has promised to give us?

And so once again, I ask: why are we so troubled by death?

---

[23] John 11:25 (ESV)

[24] Read John 10:17-18

XVII

(THE COST OF GOING HIGHER UP AND DEEPER IN)

Below is a message I sent to a friend some time ago along with a poem and its corresponding commentary I wanted her to read. Originally, I only planned to include the poem and the commentary in this book, but after writing the message, I decided it would serve as a good introduction to this concept. (The names have been removed to protect the innocent.[25])

When people think about the passage in the Gospels in which Jesus warns us to "count the cost," they usually only think about the cost of being saved; rarely, do they think about the cost of living a consistent life committed to a loving, truthful relationship with Jesus, that is, actually being one of His disciples. I think many people stop at being saved and are never truly discipled by Christ because the cost beyond simple salvation is too

---

[25] That was a joke.

71

great in their eyes. A prudent decision on their part in some sense: if it isn't worth the cost, then don't do it. But, unfortunately, the consequence of such a decision is that they miss out on so much more that could be theirs if they would just be humble and willing and if they saw that the true depths of Jesus's love is so worth it.

I'm telling you this and asking you to read the following poem and commentary because I want you to be fully aware of what it may cost you to go "higher and deeper"[26] with the LORD, my friend. Salvation costs you many things, as you well know. But God is interested in doing more in our lives than just saving us. He wants to bring us back into the depths of His holiness—back to the places where we were meant to be with Him—and He wants to restore His Image in us that was marred when we ate the forbidden fruit. And these too will cost you something. Salvation cost you something. And each time you take a step closer, higher, and deeper into His Presence, it will cost you something, not the least of which is your relationships with other people. Because, unfortunately, the truth is that not many Christians want to be any closer to God than close enough to be saved.

My friend, I have sacrificed many things and many people in my life in order to be where I am now and to have the relationship which the LORD and I share, and the list continues to grow. But I find Him more beautiful

---

[26] C.S. Lewis

and more valuable and more worthy than anything I could ever find or care to have in this life. And so, in the end, my point is simply this: count the cost of going higher up and deeper in, and you will find that He is worthy. Take heart. "Be strong and very courageous."[27] And may you never stop growing and never stop making the requisite sacrifices that are necessary to experience the fullness and the depths of the love and of the power of the Lord Jesus Christ in your heart and in your mind through the Holy Spirit. Amen.

Our Lord Jesus the Christ says to those who would
    desire Him,
"Count the cost!
Before you submit and surrender to me,
Count the cost.
For this is not the cost of abandoning possessions,
Or giving up house, or friends, or brother, or sister,
Or wife, or husband in My Name
And for the sake of the Good News.
That is not the cost about which I speak.
For the cost I speak of is far greater than the abandonment
    of relationships
Or things bought and sold.
The cost I speak of is this:
Your heart, your mind, your soul:
They are to belong to Me,

---

[27] Joshua 1:7 (ESV)

And I AM to have full and complete access to them.
You will confess your sins,
And you will repent and turn from your wicked ways.
You will humble yourself before Me and cry out,
'Father God, Lord Jesus, please! Help me!
For I am in need of Your grace and mercy!
I am in need of Your healing and restoration!'
And so I will come to you,
And I will expect you to be willing to follow through on
    your request.
For if you receive My Holy Spirit,
And yet years down the road,
You find you are still the same man or woman you
    once were,
Then is it I, the Sovereign Lord, Who was not faithful?
Is it I, The One Who Creates and Destroys, Who failed?
Is it I, The One Who Gives Rest to the Weary and Heals
    the Broken Hearted,
Who could not fully restore you?
Is it I, The Self-Existent One,
Who did not follow through on His promise of abundant
    life and freedom?
Or is it you, my dear child, who,
Having failed to count the cost before making the
    request,
Could not muster the courage and the fortitude
To allow Me to complete My work in you?
Count the cost, my dear children.
For the road is narrow, and those who find it are few,

For the path to abundant life is not easy or pain free,
And those who choose to walk it,
I will call them the greatest of My children."

"You shall be called a child of God,
And you shall receive all the benefits
And all the inheritance as the Son of God.
Through Me, you shall be accepted into the House of
  the LORD,
And you shall receive His Name,
Just as a bride receives her husband's name.
I will be in you, and you will be in Me.
Dearly Beloved, I will take you as My bride.
I will make you My wife.
I will give Myself utterly to you.
I will surrender and abandon Myself to you completely.
But if I do this, if we are to be together in such a manner,
I will expect, even more so, I will demand that you do
  the same for Me."

"Count the cost. And you will find that I AM worthy."

We do not resolve the deeper issues of our hearts, minds, and souls by pretending they are not there or by acting as if they are no longer issues simply because we "accepted Christ." Our acceptance of Christ justifies us—it frees us from the wages of sin—but it does not immediately sanctify or heal us. Sanctification and healing are together a life-long process of allowing The King deeper and deeper access into our hearts, minds, and souls through the power and the presence of the Holy Spirit. The deepest wounds and the most entrenched lies are not healed, are not restored, are not dug out of us by denying their existence, but rather by acknowledging and freely admitting them to the Body of Saints, by confessing them to Jesus, and by allowing Him entry into that part of our life. This is what shedding light on the darkness really is: allowing His light to shine on the darkness in our own hearts first.

Brothers and sisters, you do not become holy by talking about holy things; you are not healed by talking about healing; you are not restored by talking about restoration; you do not grow by talking about growth. You do become holy by talking about and confessing those areas of your life in which you are still unholy; you are healed when you surrender those areas in which you still need His healing; you are restored when you admit that your heart, mind, and soul still have need of His restoration; you grow when you acknowledge that growth is still required in significant portions of your life. For the LORD blesses those who are humble.[28]

If you want to go deeper with Jesus, then you need to allow Him to go deeper. Really deep. All the way down. Superficiality and surface-level "holy talk" will never

---

[28] This paragraph is not to be confused with self-deprecation or disparaging oneself.

lead us into the abundant life that He died to give us, a place where His truth and His love abound.

The above poem is about Jesus's expectations of us when we ask Him to truly heal and restore our hearts and minds. It is about having the courage, the faith, and the trust in His methods to deliver us into a higher and deeper understanding of His truth and His love, even when His methods scare us or cause pain. In fact, when you are dealing with He Who Gives Us Life and Makes Us Whole, sometimes pain is actually a part of the healing process and a result of His power and love working inside us. In this process, we become holy because He makes us holy. We are healed because He heals us. But even though He may bear the brunt of the workload, there is still much effort and submission required on our part; we also must take responsibility for our own growth and development. He will not do it for us because it's a relationship and a partnership, not a parasitical suckling. We are only healed and made holy when we humbly admit our lack of knowledge and understanding of Him and admit that we have nothing to give and nothing to offer Him, except that which He truly desires from us in the first place. Then, once we have humbly surrendered ourselves to Him, we need to have the courage and the fortitude to allow Him access to every single part of our lives and to allow Him to have His way with us, no matter what the cost. This is why we must first count the cost: are we sure we want to go through with this "procedure?" Because it may cost you more than you initially realized. But to receive Him fully, to be made whole and complete, to be able to walk confidently and boldly in His truth and His love, and to live the abundant life, these things are most certainly worth any cost, any price we could ever pay.

He wants YOU. Now the question is: are you willing to give Him what He wants? He wants from us and He wants us to trust Him with that which we are most afraid to give away: ourselves.

XVIII

(THE DREAMER)

A vivid imagination produces dreams of all kinds,
Dreams at all times.
I day dream, I night dream.
Big dreams, little dreams.
Exciting dreams, scary dreams.
Righteous dreams, sinful dreams.
I dream dreams that beget more dreams.
Sometimes I dream inside my dreams.
Yet all these dreams are my dreams.
All these dreams are the same dreams,
They all have the same ending.
Because when I wake up,
They were only dreams,
And I am just a man.

I am tired of dreaming my own dreams.
My dreams have no effect.
And when my eyes open,
My dreams are consumed by reality.

They carry no weight,
And they fade as quickly as they form.
What sorrow and disappointment my dreams bring,
These hollow, conglomerated shadows inside my head.

But God's dreams are dreams that can be made reality.
God dreams, and then He does.
He dreamt about creation,
And then created it.
He dreamt about you and me,
And then knit us together in darkness and seclusion.
He dreamt about the man I could be in His Kingdom,
And then breathed life into His dream,
Making the fantasy man into a real man.
I am living proof that God's dreams are more than just
dreams.

What dreams does The Dreamer dream on my behalf?
What dreams is He waiting to make reality in my life?
I am tired of dreaming my own dreams.
I want to dream God's dreams.

For thus says the LORD: "When seventy years are completed for Babylon, I will visit you, and I will fulfill to you my promise and bring you back to this place. For I know the plans I have for you, declares the LORD, plans for welfare and not for evil, to give you a future and a hope. Then you will call upon me and come and pray to me, and I will hear you. You will seek me and find me, when you seek me with all your heart. I will be found by you, declares the LORD, and I will restore your fortunes and gather you from all the nations and all the places where I have driven you, declares the LORD, and I will bring you back to the place from which I sent you into exile." Jeremiah 29:10-14 (ESV)

Trust in the LORD with all your heart, and do not lean on your own understanding. In all your ways acknowledge Him, and he will make straight your paths. Proverbs 3:5-6 (ESV)

Delight yourself in the LORD, and He will give you the desires of your heart. Psalm 37:4 (ESV)

Be still in the presence of the LORD, and wait patiently for Him to act. Psalm 37:7 (NLT)

This is the day that the LORD has made; let us rejoice and be glad in it. Psalm 118:24 (ESV)

O LORD, YOU HAVE SEARCHED ME AND KNOWN ME! You know when I sit down and when I rise up; you discern my thoughts from afar. You search out my path and my lying down and are acquainted with all my ways. Even before a word is on my tongue, behold, O LORD, YOU KNOW IT ALTOGETHER. You hem me in, behind and before, and lay your hand upon me. Such knowledge is too wonderful for me; it is high; I cannot attain it... For you formed my inward parts; you knitted me together in my mother's womb. I praise you, for I am fearfully and wonderfully made. Wonderful are your works; my soul knows it very well. My frame was not hidden from you, when I was being made in secret, intricately woven in the depths of the earth. Your eyes saw my unformed substance; in your book were written, every one of them, the days that were formed for me, when as yet there was none of them. How precious to me are your thoughts, O God! How vast is the sum of them! If I would count them, they are more than the sand. I awake, and I am still with you…Search me, O God, and know my heart! Try me and know my thoughts! And see if there be any grievous way in me, and lead me in the way everlasting! Psalm 139:1-6, 13-18, 23, 24 (ESV)

I like to make plans for myself, which is actually pretty ridiculous. It is rather difficult to make coherent, logical plans that have any hope of success when your perspective and understanding are so limited. As a human, I simply lack the knowledge or insight or breadth of vision to make plans that will properly account for all the factors and variables that go into making a decision about anything. (Except maybe to decide what I should eat for breakfast. That's generally a fairly simple endeavor.) I mean, have you ever considered all the things God must take into account when you ask Him for something? (If you haven't, you might want to give it a thought or two.) We all too often think that we ask God for things in a vacuum and that His decision on whether or not to answer in the affirmative is equally air-tight. Perhaps it is selfishness? Or maybe it is just simplicity? Maybe we just simply do not think about the fact that God's decisions on our behalves may significantly affect the other people (or the world) around us. Tracking? No? Okay, well, here are some simple examples that might help:

1) I am a man. I ask God to make Woman X my wife. Certainly there are other men who also desire Woman X to be their wife. If God gives her to me, then all those other men cannot also have her. How does God decide which man is best suited to be Woman X's husband? How does God decide what would be best for His plans, His glory, His Kingdom, His children? (Unless, of course, no one in this scenario even gives God a say in the matter, and everyone just decides for themselves, which is also quite typical.)

2) You ask God to bless your business with financial prosperity and lots of customers. Well, even though there are quite a few people on Earth, at the end of the day, the number is still finite. So who gets enough of the customers for their business to be successful? And this isn't even taking into account whether you have a good product or not. It's kind of hard to bless crap, you know?

Side bar: on the topic of presenting a good product to the masses, we should desire to be excellent for Jesus.

We should desire to use the gifts, talents, abilities, and passions He has designed into us to their utmost degree. But let's face it. Sometimes our passions and our talents don't necessarily line up too well. Not everyone who plays baseball ends up in the MLB. And not every chef ends up with their own cooking show. Some people are very passionate about things they are not very good at. So be wise in the pursuit of your dreams and learn to evaluate yourself with a sober mind. If your cooking skills are not up to par, perhaps it is best you do not try to open your own restaurant at which you are the head chef.

Of course, there are also a lot of really good baseball players out there who are perfectly content to coach rather than shoot for the big leagues. And many home cooks are satisfied to bless their family and friends with ridiculously tasty pastries (which rhymes) rather than open their own pastry shop in downtown La Jolla, CA, where they could have charged rich folks three times as much for their baked delights as they would have had they opened their shop a few miles up the road in Oceanside. Conclusion: if you are passionate about something, enjoy the bananas out of it and do it to the utmost of the ability God has given you. Use your passion for that something as a way to connect with other people, especially unbelievers. And if God has seen fit to also bless you with great talent to match your passion, then "do all things unto the glory of God."[29] This

---

[29] 1 Corinthians 10:31

is very pleasing to Him…Side bar complete…Actually, one last thing: if anyone out there decides to use "The Tasty Pastry" as the name for their pastry shop, you'll have to get with my lawyers (who are imaginary and don't even have law degrees); we'll negotiate a reasonable settlement.

3) I ask God for a bright, sunny day so I can have a picnic with my boo. A local farmer is praying for plenty of rain so his crops will grow and his harvest will be bountiful. Need I ask the question at this point?

These three scenarios are all relatively simple, and they only involve a relatively small number of people. Zoom out, big picture style: how does God decide which nations to bless and which to judge and put in their place? Much bigger scale, much more complex, many more people involved. Oh, and by the way, He isn't just the God of our tiny planet. How about the God of all the Heavens and the Earth and everything in between? Angels and demons. Supernovas and nebulas. Amoebas and orangutans. Are you understanding the point I am making? Fantastic. Needless to say, He has a lot on His plate. But no need to worry. He is a big God. He can handle it all and then some. And what's better is that He is good, and He loves you.

Or here is another way of looking at dreams. Sometimes we have aspirations for our lives. We have passions and desires, many of which truly have been designed into us by God. But it is also true that "for everything there is a season, and a time for every matter under heaven."[30] Sometimes He only wants to use things for a particular season in our lives. And then, seasons change, and it is time to move on to another dream.

I wanted to be a professional baseball player so badly growing up, and I still have such a tremendous passion for the game. But some time in high school seasons changed, and I had to let go of that dream. I am so thankful that He took baseball away from me. Because if He had not taken away *that* experience, then I would have completely missed out on everything I *did* experience. And through these experiences, I have learned that submitting to His will and His desires for my life is far more pleasurable and fulfilling than leading my own way. I have learned that sometimes I need to let go of *my* dreams in order to make room for *God's* dreams. And I have learned that when I sacrifice my dreams for the sake of His dreams, I never really sacrifice anything at all. For when I delight myself in the LORD, He gives me the desires of my heart,[31] and I realize that His dreams for me and my dreams for myself have become one and the same.

---

[30] Ecclesiastes 3:1 (ESV)
[31] Psalm 37:4

XIX

(THE STRENGTH OF GOD IN A MAN)

I believe I figured out why women are so obsessed with the 50 Shades of Grey series: strength. Men are attracted to the beauty in women, and women are attracted to the strength in men. The problem is that most women's beauty is superficial, and most men's strength is counterfeit. Most women's beauty is actually pride and vanity; their beauty only goes "skin deep" and does not go down into their heart. Most men's strength only appears to be strength because of how rough and vulgar it is. In reality, it is prideful or arrogant posturing as an attempt to hide or to overcome their insecurities. Weak women—and, unfortunately, many stronger women too—are attracted to this apparent strength because they are fooled into thinking it is the real deal. They are fooled because they know not what authentic manhood (true strength) looks like; because they know not what authentic womanhood (true beauty) looks like; because they know not the Father who created them: The Author and Originator of both beauty and strength.

The character, Christian Grey, is unusually alluring and appealing to women because he seems to display so much strength. He is powerful and dominant. He is charismatic, and he controls his environment absolutely. His behavior fosters a false sense of safety and security in the women he manipulates. They are drawn in by the seduction of illusory strength. But what appears to be strong is, in fact, sinister: he utilizes these strong qualities to hypnotize his prey while he selfishly takes what he wants, and then leaves the women questioning and confused.

Power, dominance, control. These are indeed qualities of strength. But true strength, godly strength, directs these towards oneself, not towards others. These qualities are leveraged for discipline, not for manipulation. Strength rules himself, not those around him.

Ladies, allow your men to exercise true strength, and stop expecting them to be beautiful and tame. Gentlemen, demand your women let beauty penetrate past their skin and into their hearts and minds, and stop utilizing what little strength you do have for selfish gain and abuse. Strength is meant for selflessness, not selfishness.

Boys and girls, little boys and little girls, it is time we have the courage to grow up. For the strength of God in a man is Proverbs 16:32 (ESV):

"Whoever is slow to anger is better than the mighty, and he who rules his spirit [is better] than he who takes a city."

XX

(无限/LIMITLESS)

心脑灵无限
每一天改变
前后不样脸
自世鬼面前
心脑灵无限

A heart, mind, and soul without limits.
Everyday a transformation.
Before and after: a different man.
In the face of myself, the world, and the devil,
My heart, mind, and soul are limitless.

How can I speak of being limitless when I feel limited in so many ways?

I would very much like to be a husband, but I am limited here. There is a whole realm of relational intimacy that is still a complete mystery to me. I want to experience this beautiful aspect of life that continues to be kept away, but it is something I cannot give to myself, and the One who can give withholds.

I want to grow and to mature and to increase each day, but even much of my personal growth is dependent upon God's revelation and timing. Some of His mysteries I am incapable of comprehending until He reveals them to me through life experience or until I have learned some other lesson that then gives me the capacity to understand the next; they are building blocks, and I am not the One who stacks them. Though the student may be sharp enough to self-instruct in some areas, there is a reason why we have teachers and mentors. We need someone greater than us to explain those things which are beyond us. I am at the mercy of His lesson plan, though I often try to be my own instructor.

But there is more to it, something much darker and more sinister than marital status and lesson plans: fire, worms, gnashing of teeth. It is the devil. He has deceived me into joining his rebellion. I want to grow and to increase. But the more I grow, the greater my capacity becomes, and the more limited I feel. I feel limited by myself and my imperfections. I feel limited by other people, by their fear and lack of understanding. My body limits me. My circumstance limits me. My location limits me. Even my own God limits me. He continues to withhold things from me which I greatly desire to have. He keeps me in this condition of neediness and dependence when all I want is perfection and a sinless nature so I can live the kind of life I was supposed to be able to live when He designed humanity. Is that not what He wants from me? But it is not. He has set me in this place and in this condition because He wants me to be reliant upon His grace and His mercy. He wants me to be in need of His forgiveness. He wants the fullness of His loving character manifested for me to see. For if I needed not His love, how would I ever know it?

But this is where the rebellion begins and where the fire of Hell consumes. I want to do and to be more than what He is allowing me to do and to be. And that is called pride. My initial thoughts on this matter were that I do not want to overthrow God. I just want to be unlimited or de-limited—I want to be allowed to become everything I want to be. However, the logical conclusion of this mindset is that if I keep growing and expanding my capacity, eventually the only One who would be in my way *is* God. And so, naturally, at that point, if pride were to grip me, and if eliminating limitations were to become the overriding directive in my life, then I would want to eliminate or to overthrow even Him.

This, then, is the darkness and the evil within me: I want to be God. I want to be my own god. I want God to stop holding me back. I want my power to be greater than His so He can't limit me anymore. I am like Satan—deceived into thinking anyone could ever be greater. Like my original father and mother before me, I have chosen to adopt the creed of this Great Liar and of his insurrection against the God of Israel. And yet, He has made Himself just that: "The God of those who struggle against Him."[32] In my revolt, He has made Himself My King all the same.

What resolution will bring peace to this Kingdom? How can I become greatness and excellence without trying to depose Him? Rebellion leads to death. Mere acceptance seems depressing and bitter. I propose a hybrid answer. Finding balance is the key. This is my final conclusion: I will seek to remove as many limitations as possible while joyfully and humbly accepting the ones I have no power, or ability, or opportunity to change. When I have adopted this attitude, the challenge then becomes discerning which limitations can be removed and which must become my joy and my humility.

2 Corinthians 12:1-10

In Christ, I am limitless. Because He is limitless in me.

---

[32] The word *Israel* in Hebrew means "struggles against God."

Printed in the United States
By Bookmasters